DISCOVERING
GOD'S
Presence

John Gillette's writings flow from a lifetime of experience. It is one thing to write out of a knowledge based on research. It is an entirely different thing to write out of a depth of life experience. John has both. As a pastor who has cared for the needs of a congregation, as a husband who has experienced the tragic loss of a wife, and as a child of God who has walked through the joys and pain of following the Lord, John has so much to offer in this series. From the opening pages, through to the very end, you will be blessed by the insights, loving tone, and encouragement you receive from this series. God has used John in ministry and will continue to use him through this life-giving series.

—*Josh Mateer, D. Min.*

True, illustrative, practical stories are like windows that unlock Bible truths and promises. Along with a masterfully orchestrated short stories should come the truth that God's Word and love has been experienced by His servants as they partner with Him in the work of rebuilding the Kingdom. A gifted teacher, Dr. Gillette lives an ordinary life abiding in Christ and being an obedient servant of the Lord. As he sees God working in his life, and in the lives of those to whom he ministers, his faith is refreshing, and he is encouraged to press on through life's uncertainties.

Only a lifetime dedicated to nurturing, ministering, teaching, and keen insight though the power of the Holy Spirit, can produce such poignant stories that teach and challenge.

—*Mulonge M. Kalumbula, Ph.D.*

John's books give us hope and light. He reminds us that through Jesus we are never alone. I have certainly needed that reminder in my life and in my practice. In holding a patient's hand, and helping them through a condition or disease, reminding them that they are never alone has become the greatest gift of health care.

—*Linda M. Kunce, D.C.*

The series reminds me that Jesus knows what it is like to live in a human body. I have received Jesus and His forgiveness, but as the book suggests, I also have the power from the Holy Spirit. His books have encouraged me to gain courage through prayer and confidence is Jesus to meet my needs. John's honesty is very special to read as he reflects on his own life and struggles. I like his explanation that "the soul is where the emotions are, and the mind is where the thinking takes place." It's been good for me to read that God works through weakness and learn that John found God with him in the middle of struggle.

—*Arvid W. Vandyke, Ed.D.*

Discovering God's counsel is a book full of great spiritual truths from someone who has developed a very close and deep relationship with Jesus through his life. John provides a meaningful and inspirational testimony, with examples from his own experiences, of how relying on God's Word and promises can give you the power, hope, and peace you need to overcome life's struggles and challenges. The Scriptures he chose in his book were on a point and helpful. It was an enjoyable and wonderful read.

—*Thoa Reyna, J.D.*

John has written a user-friendly and practical series for anyone desiring to live beyond the superficial and venture into the supernatural. The world needs this *Pastoral Health Care* series. Pastors and followers of Jesus need the insights from John's lifetime experience of walking with God and caring for His people through the power of the Holy Spirit. John has brilliantly show that God is enough, God's counsel is enduring, and God reigns supremely. This important series will serve both the church and the world for many years to come.

—*Kizombo Kalumbula, Jr., Ph.D.*

John Gillette's inspirational book *Glorify God* is a fantastic reminder of how I should approach each day and how blessed I am. It is so easy to get caught up in the hustle and bustle of today's lifestyle and forget what is really important. John's encouraging words are a great reminder of how we all should live each day. I have a great foundation of faith, but John's book helps me to remember what is important and allows me to reflect on the wonderful things I have and to be gracious to God for those blessings.

— *Tammy Thelen, Au.D., CCC-A*

John's book contains a lifetime of experiences guided by the law of the Bible, which reaches an important spiritual conclusion. This book is written to open your mind and self– consciousness to the Holy Spirit, which in turn provides a path to salvation. The book draws the reader closer to personal observation which provides reasoning to exact reference to scripture. Highly recommended for self-development of Christian faith."

—*Nicholas A. Reyna, Esq.*

FANTASTIC
FAVORITES
PART 1

DISCOVERING
GOD'S
Presence

*What does it mean to live
in Jesus Christ?*

JOHN F. GILLETTE

Chapbook Press

Schuler Books

2660 28th Street SE

Grand Rapids MI 49512

www.schulerbooks.com/chapbook-press

Fantastic Favorites Book Series Part One

Discovering God's Presence: What does it mean to live in Jesus Christ?

Copyright ©2023 — John F. Gillette. All rights reserved. Published 2023.

Printed at Schuler Books, Chapbook Press, Grand Rapids, Michigan, in the United States of America.

Distribution contact:at jjgillette@comcast.net.

ISBN 13: 9781957169583

Library of Congress Control Number: 2023916528

Cover photo: Paige Weber/Unsplash

Cover Design: Frank Gutbrod Graphic Design

Printed in the United States of America

Books by John Gillette:

Pastoral Health Care

Discovering God's Sufficiency
Going Beyond Ourselves and Experiencing the Supernatural
Part One

Discovering God's Love
Confirming God's Love Through the Evidence of Historical Facts
Part Two

Discovering God's Counsel
Applying His Spiritual Solution to Meet Difficult Trials
Part Three

Discovering God's Kingdom
Finding a Way to Understand Ourselves in a Complex World
Part Four

Discovering God's Heart
Finding God's Heart Pulse is Our Daily Challenge
Part Five

Divine Dialogue

Glorify God
Christianity is a Divine Vitality
Part One

Dynamic Doer
Biblical Christianity is Jesus Christ
Part Two

Satisfying Strength
Biblical Meditation Works — Allow Psalms to Sweep You into All Directions
Part Three

Disciplining Dynamics
Christian Counseling Teaching Tools
Part Four

Celebrate Christ
Above All Christ
Part Five

Fantastic Favorites

Discovering God's Presence

What does it mean to life in Jesus Christ?

Part One

Discovering God's Eternal Life

What have I learned about Jesus Christ?

Part Two

Discovering God's Supernatural Activities

Why Do I Believe in Jesus Christ?

Part Three

Discovering God's Favor

What is my personal testimony concerning Jesus Christ?

Part Four

Discovering God's Church

How did Jesus Christ's church begin?

Part Five

Joy and John Gillette

I t is with great affection that I dedicate this book series to my wife Joy, who radiated God's grace. We wrote the Pastoral Healthcare Series together. Applying God's spiritual solutions to meet us in difficult trials has become even more practical in my life with the recent death of my dear wife, Joy.

This book has been reproduced in her memory while the content is the same, my dedication has become more personal than ever before. The separation is painful, but as I gather my suffering and feelings of incompleteness, I will succeed with God's peace and presence. The guidelines of this book have brought blessing to our life together. We have pursued them with great persistence. I am assured she is in God's presence rejoicing and at peace. I will be with her to experience God's eternal presence someday as well. " . . . Blessed are they who put their trust in him." (Psalm 2:12)

Table of Contents

Absolutes

When I say the word "suffer," it makes me cringe. I am going to seek to escape the reality of pain in my life through television, business, entertainment, or drugs. Suffering does not fit with the world's notion of success or the theology of some people in regard to God's goodness and victorious living in Christ.

These words have started the process:

Disease—discomfort

Discouragement—depression

Death—dread

I decided to face life and health realistically and with absolutes. I am learning to live every moment in God's presence. Please keep in mind that we do not suffer apart from the knowledge of God. Do not be intimidated by all the talk. God knows all the details . . . read and receive confidence through Matthew 10:29-31. Keep in mind in whom you have believed in and trusted your body, soul, and spirit to. Obtain confidence through 2 Timothy 1:12. Keep in mind God's character rather than his creation. Read Genesis 21:33, Isaiah 40:13-14, Ephesians 1:3-14, and Proverbs 19:6. He is in control. Keep in mind the big picture and let it rule your life—not the suffering. Keep in mind the power source—Ephesians 5:18. Keep going forward with inner confidence—I Peter 5:10, 4:13.

This is written to help me and you. I know it works because I have experienced the spiritual solution growth process. It is not a formula, remedy, prescription, or cure. It will help in the deepest hour. Digest it into your blood stream. Allow the key thoughts to penetrate your being. Your inner being must be guided by the Holy Spirit. He will cause the victory. Instead of being on the bottom of the mountain creeping slowly upward, you can be at the top looking down on victory.

A lot can be said about suffering, sickness, and unknown health issues. This is simply the course I have followed and will continue to follow in order to conquer. It takes team effort for me to conquer. Every day I have to affirm, adjust, and accept God's plan of action.

As far as I am concerned, the Bible is absolute in truth. You do not have to agree but travel with me in my journey. You do not have anything to lose. Perhaps you will find the answers that I have found. In my deepest worry and concern, I have been trained to look to the Holy Scriptures for answers. They have proved themselves as a profitable resource. With the Holy Spirit's guidance through them. I have discovered peace and rest when I did not think I could be able to. Therefore, in my recent struggle to obtain right-thinking (Biblical thinking), I began reading in the Old Testament Book of Psalms. There were times I could not read, meditate, think, or pray. God knew my circumstances and gave me little bits and pieces to chew on. Later I was able to go deeper with each word and grasp God's awesome meaning. In Psalm 100:3, God says, "He made me, and I am his." The three words penetrated my spirit, soul, and body and in that order. Sometimes I would think only on the "three words". If God made me and he did, he certainly cares about what he made. I am not left alone in this misery. He knows my limitations, and he is in control. He has my best in mind.

I was excited to know that little two letter words can mean a lot. I was able to build upon that phrase in Psalm 100:3. My life verse in Psalm 16:8 provided an outline to the text. His power, presence, and peace kept ringing in my ears. I am thankful for grandparents, parents, personal family, years of training and colleagues that have paved the way.

According to the Apostle Peter (I Peter 2:25) and The Apostle Paul (Acts 13:35), Psalm 16 relates to Christ. It expresses his feeling of human emotion. During his suffering and death, he called on God to preserve him. The first verse gives a brief but deep description of the character of his entire walk on earth. "O God in thee do I put my trust' (v1). The last verse is a summary of his path of life "at thy presence is fullness of joy" (v11). From my childhood, I have followed Jesus. My desire is the same as his. "O God in thee do I put my trust" V1. In good and bad days, I want to experience continual strength, support, and steadfastness provided by him.

I discovered Psalm 16 in my teens. I was graduating from high school and was asked by my church to share a personal testimony. I prayed for a verse that would become my constant companion through life. God gave me Psalm 16:8. it has lifted me up and has helped me to confront my weaknesses. My prayer is "thy will be done." My favorite verse gave me the goal and foundation to build upon. Praising him moved me from the negative to the positive.

"I have set the Lord always before me, because he is at my right hand, I shall not be moved" (Psalm 16:8). I know this refers to the testimony of Jesus Christ. My loyalty is given to him. He is my model to follow. In the first phrase, "I have set the Lord always before me" gives me continued strength. In my inadequacy, I praise God for his inheritance. I belong to him, and he is my Savoir and Lord. I am his heir and I have a great inheritance. I belong to his kingdom (Matthew 25:34.) I have citizenship on earth and heaven. My stay down here is short and is directed through my eternal destiny. It is a decision of trust. I am able to overcome all of my inadequacies because I belong to the King. He provides the way. It is possible because of his death (Hebrews 9:15). In his death, he took care of the sin problem. My sin is forgiven. "I have come short of his glory" (Romans 3:23). He provides the way (John 14:6) to be a part of his family (John 1:12). The Holy Spirit has sealed it (Ephesians 1:13-14). He placed his approval and authority on it. No one can remove the seal. Since I am in Christ, I have been transformed (I Corinthians 15:50-53). Since he has given me faith (Galatians 3:18,22) I can and will overcome. I have been promised continual strength that flows into my bloodstream through the Holy Spirit.

Praise God for his goodness extended to me. I have reached out to him. "Thou art my Lord . . . I take delight in you" (Psalm 16:2,3). In doing this, I have learned that he has created the initial desire. He is always near, "He is at my right hand" (Psalm 16:8). I have to relearn that God causes all things to work together for good to those who love him (Romans 8:28). I live in a contaminated world, and it rubs off. Bad things will happen, and I cannot stop them. Creation was completely good when it came from God's hand. I have to remember that the negative never has the last word.

I praise God for his counsel given to me. Communion with the Holy Spirit has been instructive and encouraging. God is near when you feel him and when you don't feel him. He is there when I sense hm and when I don't sense him. He counsels with his promises that he is going to accomplish something whether I think so or not. My negatives are part of his positive program. God knows where he wants to take me and how he wants to get me there. He is my support.

The last part of the verse says, "I shall not be moved" (Psalm 16:8). This has brought the promise of continued steadfastness. I praise God for his preservation. He has the power working in me that makes my heart beat. In spite of my sensitivity which sometimes creates a hindrance, he enables me. God's power is very personal. I may not know what to think or ask but he can do it because he is able. His grace is sufficient to meet the need (2 Corinthians 9:8). I can develop firmness but also have a soft heart. God will keep me from stumbling and make me stand in his presence blameless and with great joy (Jude 24). In him I put trust for eternity.

I praise God for his hope (Psalm 16:9). I have discovered that I am secure in the Lord. No matter what happens, he is near. If God is for me, who can be against me? (Romans 8:31,32). God loves me and he is aware of every detail. No tribulation, distress, or persecution will separate me for him (Romans 8:35). I can have complete rest in him. He will keep my heart safe. I will not be shaken.

Repeat v8 with me and between each phrase, recite its meaning. I am convinced that as I praise God through this scripture, I will live with his power, presence, and peace or strength, support and steadfastness. This verse would become my model to follow. It has stayed with me all these years (over eighty) without failing me once. It gives input to Psalm 100:3 which has become a recourse of power for current spirit, soul, and body adjustments. The Bible says "He made me and I am his" (Psalm 100:3). I think the promise of power will be produced in my life as I affirm the Scripture as a solution growth process.

The process of growth begins with understanding the "He" in the text. It is going to take time and we must learn "to be still" (Psalm 46:10). The scripture says, "be still and know that I am God." Knowing God requires time alone with him, the word meditation in a broad sense means to chew something. God wants us to chew his word up and allow it to digest into our bloodstream. God is unique and he is one of a kind. We cannot compare him to anyone else. Nothing else in the universe is like him. We understand God on his terms. He will provide understanding. Yet through his characteristics, he can be known. Each characteristic will provide us with power. Our driving force should be found in his attributes.

I realize that we are limited but his whole personhood (the Trinity) will make him knowable. This definitely is a meaningful pursuit. Just think of it . . . "people who know God will display strength and take action." (Daniel 11:32). Confidence, security, wisdom, grace, peace, power, and authority will become a part of our lives. God is invisible. We see the reality of God in what he does, not in what he looks like.

The "He" is God. We have authority because he is sovereign. He has absolute rule and control over all of his creation. God rules absolutely the affairs of men. He does what he pleases, and he can do whatever he wants because it is all his (Psalm 24:1). Things do not just happen. Everything that occurs does so under the hand of a sovereign God. There is no chance happening, no luck, no mistakes, and both good and bad fall under his control. "I can do all things through Him who strengthens me" (Philippians 4:13). Our lives are empowered through him. We are totally dependent upon his supply. We can live with authority because he is in charge, and we belong to him.

The "He" is God. We have authority because he has perfect knowledge. God's knowledge is intuitive. God knows what he knows simply because he knows it. (Isaiah 40:13-14). Nothing can be hidden from God (Hebrews 4:13). "The eyes of the Lord are in every place watching the evil and the good." (Proverbs 15:3). His comprehensive knowledge is able to give us authority in our daily lives. (Psalms 139:1-2). God knows how we think (Ezekiel 11:5). He knows and understands every thought and intent of the heart (Isaiah 16:7). He is intimately acquainted with all my ways (Psalm 139:3). Our lives are empowered though him because he chose us in him before the foundation of the world that we should be holy and blameless before him. In love he predetermined us to adoption as sons . . . to the praise of the glory of his grace (Ephesians 1:4-6). God does what he does on purpose. We have so many limitations. We can live with authority because he is the all-knowing, all wise, all–loving God.

The "He" is God. We have authority because there is nothing he cannot do. His unlimited power reflects his divine glory and accomplishes his sovereign will. He uses his power to magnify his glory and accomplish his perfect will. "Power belongs to God" (Psalm 62:11). "Great is our Lord and abundant in strength" (Psalm 137:5). He has self-generating power. God never needs anything outside of himself. Our lives are empowered through him because we are able through his grace to "be filled up to all the fullness of God" Ephesians 3:19-20). We are able to do exceedingly abundantly beyond all that we ask or think, according to the power that works within us. We can be assured in our total dependence upon him that we can live with authority because he is all powerful. I can't Lord, but you can.

The "He" is God. We have authority because he is everywhere present. God is spirit; therefore, he exists everywhere at the same time. God is present everywhere in all the fullness of his deity. The Bible says that "He is in you" (I John 4:4). He is everywhere equally all the time. "In him we live and move and exist" (Acts 17:28). Our bodies are his residence on this earth (I Corinthians 6:19). Our lives are empowered through him because he lives inside of us and supplies all our needs according to his riches in glory in Christ Jesus (Philippians 4:19). We can assured in our total dependence upon him because he is everywhere present.

It is no wonder that we can "shout aloud with joy" because we are able to love with the promise of power. In knowing God and possessing him brings empowerment. "All the earth and to all generations" are able to do the same if they know that the Lord is God. We are able to have a relationship with God through his son Jesus. Complete assurance of the truth has to take place (John 14:6). The name Lord refers to his supreme personal intelligence.

Are we able to say, "we are his people and the sheep of his pasture?" If he has become our shepherd and an intimate relationship has taken place through faith, we can enter into his gates with thanksgiving. His kingdom provides spiritual guidance as mercy, truth, righteousness, peace, harmony, etc. The "He" that has made us and not we ourselves has made it possible for us to live with power and shout with praise.

The Bible says, "He has made me, and I am his." (Psalm 100:3). In understanding the "He" will bring illumination to the meaning of "me". The "He" lives in us. The entire godhead (Trinity) dwells in us. The scripture teaches that God the Father (Ephesians 4:6), that God the Son (Colossians 1:27), and God the Spirit (I Corinthians 6:19) are present within us. Christians have possession of the divine nature. This is truly a mystery. The individual person of the godhead lives and work through us (Romans 8:9). The "I in you" refers to the Trinity. The believer is in Christ and Christ is in the believer. The sole condition is abiding in Christ. Our position in Christ is neither attained nor maintained. It is accomplished through the power of God through grace. Abiding means to make the right adjustment between yourself and Christ (John 15:10). This is not fulfilled though self-promotion. It depends only on faith. Self-development sounds good but the victorious life is through a "walk in the spirit" (Galatians 5:16). It is not actually, the walk but our yieldedness to the Spirit. The key word is adjustment. The sin problem and its power over us is taken care of at the cross through Christ's death. In his resurrection, we are enabled to walk every day and conquer sin in our lives.

God himself has determined the desire of the heart. The outworking of those desires will be according to his own energizing power. The pure grace of God brings about fruitfulness. Our response: "yield yourselves unto God, as those that are delivered from the dead and your members as instruments of righteousness unto God" (Romans 6:13).

"If any man be in Christ, he is a new creation, old things are passed away, behold, all things are becomes new" (2 Corinthians 5:17). How do we live out the "in Christ" focus of this text? In John 14, Jesus says that the Holy Spirit would be our aid to live "in Christ" and dependence on him would take place. I am concerned with the "old things are passed away" and the new things taking their place. It seems like some adjustments need to take place. The key is "abide in me and I in you" (John 15:21). I am glad that the little word "in" is found here. I am assured that it is possible to obtain success in my walk because the power of the walk is through God.

Absolute deity is at work. I need to know what it means to "abide in me." When we get served from the vine, our life is lost. We become weak and empty. We stop allowing the indwelling Christ to be his work in us. We are not abiding in the true vine but ourselves or some other dependency.

In verse 3 and 7 of John 15 the first adjustment given is our thinking. "Abide in Christ" means to abide in his Word. Abiding and believing God's Word are interwoven. His word has to become saturated into our mind. We will think right when we think with his mind. This is a huge statement. What it simply means is to memorize the scripture and apply it to everything in life.

Closely related to this is the needed manifestation and result of "abiding in Christ and his Word"—obedience. Verse 10 states that "if you keep my commandments, ye shall abide in my love." There is no exception. Obedience involves yieldedness in him. Remember he is the vine, and we are the branches. The second adjustment is to obey what he says concerning your circumstances. Make a list of the disturbing facts that hound your life and see what he says about them. Then act and make a decision to remove the "old things" and replace them with the "new things". This might be difficult because sometimes we like to hold onto the old ways, or it may be that we need help to understand what needs to be removed and replaced.

The adjustment business involves the recognition by the believer that the outworking's are God's, not our own. "For without me, you can do nothing" (verse 5). God is the vine. The branches cannot make it on their own. The fruit–bearing sap flowing into us comes from God. Prayer is a part of the adjustment process. If we "abide in Christ" that is to say that we abide in his Word, abide in obedience, abide in discipline, and abide in his authority, we will "ask what ye will, and it shall be done unto you" (verse 7). Abiding in Christ is praying in his will and having results—including more much fruit. This is the third adjustment. The Christ walk is difficult at times yet very rewarding at times. Keep in mind your relationship with God will not be broken but your fellowship can be reduced. Make the daily adjustment and "abide in Christ."

The Bible says, "He has made me, and I am his" (Psalm 100:3). He has made me. He lives within me. He cares for me. I have discovered a tremendous promise. "Have mercy upon me O Lord; for I am weak. O Lord, heal me . . ." (Psalm 6:2). The cry is for physical and spiritual well-being. God is not against me when I suffer. He cares about me enough to save every one of my tears. (Psalm 56:8). Through the tears, "he has heard my supplication, the Lord will receive my prayer." (Psalm 6:9). God says, "He who dwelleth in the secret place of the most high shall abide under the shadow of the Almighty. I will say of the Lord, he is my refuge and my fortress, my God in him will I trust" (Psalm 91:1-2). The great promise is for you and me if we believe. Yet the promise is not made to all who believe but only to those who are willing to make their abode in the secret place. This means to sit down or take up residence there. The word 'abide' refers to constant and continuous dwelling and not just a temporary visitation during trouble. My assurance of comfort is through Jesus Christ who is the secret place of the Most High. His hand is covering me.

One way this is possible is through understanding the awesomeness of God. He is beyond my comprehension. Recently I was watching a DVD and a young man shard many delightful facts about astronomy, science, and physiology. I was reminded once again of God's greatness. I discovered that God is not on the outer edge of the universe, nor does he belong in a specimen jar. I can celebrate God's self-revelation and grandeur up close and personal. I can also seek to to address an appropriate response to him.

I am quite aware of the fact that we do not live in a bed of roses. Hardships do come to us. Many of our problems are a direct result of human failure. We are accountable for our failures, and we suffer their consequences. Sometimes we suffer because our bodies are preparing to return to the dust from which it came. Sometimes our suffering may be a means to display God's power and prove our love and loyalty to him.

When we say the word 'suffer', it makes us cringe. We are going to seek to escape the reality of pain in our lives any way we can . . . television, busyness, entertainment, drugs. Suffering does not fit with the world's notion of success or the theology of God's goodness and victorious living in Christ. Why must I suffer? I really don't feel well. I have been told that God is absolutely good and infinitely loving. He is all-powerful but why do I suffer if I am a product of his creative power and the focus of his infinite love? I don't understand!

I am not alone; a lot of people suffer. I wish it would come to an end . . . you know what I mean . . . an instant cure. I realize God has permitted suffering. He knew that the plan he chose, even though it allowed for sin and suffering, ultimately would bring about the greatest good and glory. Out suffering is directly related to the curse that came that came upon the earth as the result of sin. With sin came corruption, suffering, and death. This is not to say that every occurrence of suffering in our lives is direct punishment for our personal sins. The sooner we accept the reality that we are living in a fallen world with its suffering, the sooner we will be able to get on with living effectively.

As God takes up residence in me, I begin to live in his shadow and experience his hand covering me. Comfort is a result of continuous dwelling in him. It has helped me to study God's attributes. It is not possible to fully define or understand God, but we can gain confidence in our limited understanding. He is self-existent, self-sufficient, eternal, and controller of all things. He knows the worst and the best about us, and he knows what he is going to make us. He hath abounded toward us in all wisdom . . . knowing his own will and purpose. It has helped me to know the facts. Fear is dreadful, but fear in God is hopeful. "The Lord is my light and salvation, whom shall I fear?" (Psalm 27:1). My anxiety, tension, and uneasiness lessens when I think-right. I have had to identify the problem I have had to commit it to the Lord through being more aware of him than the sickness. I have had to release it to him because he is quite able to handle it. I have had to stand firm and not retreat in my decision. His word must be implanted in my mind and heart. I am able to think-right when Jesus Christ is personalized in my life. How does that happen? I must acknowledge my lost condition. As a sinner, I do not measure up to his standards. The consequence of sin is death and that emphasizes separation from God. God loved us and gave us his son to be our substitute—to die on the cross, to shed his blood—so the sin debt could be paid. We appropriate this forgiveness by a single act of faith. Have you believed and received Jesus into your heart? If not, just admit your sin and ask him to come into your life and take him at his word?

It has helped me to be intimate with the Lord. A conscious continuous fellowship is necessary. I am surrounded with his protection, no matter what happens. A daily breathing out of sin through confession and breathing in of his presence is necessary. This, of course, involves self-examination with truth, submission, and identification with the Lord, along with asking and believing with thanksgiving. Intimacy with God through Christ is the Holy Spirit is accomplished through constant trust. This trust is of great value and benefit. It provides that inner assurance that is needed to keep going. Work on each step and the result will be confidence, strength, peace, and joy.

It has helped me to know that the Holy Spirit makes intercession for me as well as Jesus Christ. When I cannot read scripture, pray, or even accept the comfort of others, I am assured that I am not left to my own resources. He keeps on helping me. He knows my needs and my very mind and heart. He knows the end from the beginning, and he knows what is necessary, He intercedes to enable me to meet each crisis. He prays according to God's plans for my life. It is God who makes all things work together in our lives for good. It has helped me in weakness to not complain. I discredit the name of Jesus when I do. In sickness, I resolve to do my best and to be bright in my activities, It is easy to be negative depressed, and discouraged, but I try to count my blessings which are many. Accepting support from others is helpful and necessary also.

Many thoughtful ideas have been presented. Do the ideas work? Is it theory? Does it really happen? Many years ago, as a teenager, I did a good Samaritan thing in defending someone in school. The result of that kindness ended up with infection in my hands. The doctors tried medicine to cure the infection, but it did not work. Then they tried radiation in my treatment which did not work either. The third treatment was acid placed on the infection to eat it away. This was the most painful and I could feel the acid eat away the infection and surrounding flesh. During this treatment, I remember reciting every scripture verse I could possibly remember. I rehearsed the fallen nature of man and my position in "Christ". I evaluated my relationship with God, made confession, and submitted to God, my body, soul, and spirit. When I did not know what else to do, I just simply gave myself over to the Holy Spirit's interceding power. I placed my focus on Jesus and the little song, "Jesus Loves Me." I kept repeating it until the presence of his person seemed to lift me up. My one hand was touched by Jesus and the other with the Holy Spirit. I thanked my heavenly father for placing me in his shadow. The doctors had to operate and surgically remove the infection. My faith was stretched, and I know I had been visited by the Almighty.

Sometimes it is harder to stand on the outside looking in. When loved ones experience suffering and pain, I have worried and anxiety has set in. Facing illnesses and weaknesses are not easy (cancer, heart disease, diabetes). With my Biblical studies and experiences, I found myself pacing the halls of a hospital. I have been in the hospital many times visiting others and I display compassion and give a sense of confidence. The assurance of God's presence and mercy was always shared. This assurance of God's presence and mercy was always shared. This was different. These people belonged to me; I would rather take their place. God had something to teach me.

I had to give myself a swift kick because with my actions, I was doubting God's sufficiency. I looked at one of my pastoral prescription cards and was reminded of God's attributes. I began to recite them before too long, I was so full of thinking about God's superiority, sovereignty, and sufficiency that I thanked him for the experience. He is totally responsible for all of creation (Colossians 1:15-16). He has life within himself (John 5:26). God has self-generating power. What he chooses to do and not to do is up to him. My loved one was placed in God's sovereign hand. We have to learn to love our lives in the awareness of his sovereignty. God says, "I am God, you are man; you don't tell me, I tell you." When we cannot see him, acknowledge him, recognize him. Whether we do or don't, he is going to be God. In my hospital pacing, I decided to be dependent on him and not myself. My feeling of apprehension, uneasiness, concern, worry, dread, and anxiety came under the shadow of the Almighty.

Trusting God becomes easy when you practice it on a daily basis. The songwriter wrote, "I know not what the future holds but I know who holds the future." I believe that dwelling in the secret place of the Most High and abiding under the shadow of the Almighty has to take place in good or bad health. He has become my fortress because of the trust he provided. Let's keep in mind that God's ways often are beyond the capacity of out human ability to understand. He provides the strength when we need it and in the way he wants to. Sometimes anger, frustration, and disappointment appear but my hope is not based on an emotionally based fantasy of what might happen but a hope that is based solidly on the Biblical teaching about God and the universe. Consider all the mighty works of his hand—he is able. We are in his shadow and can find peace and comfort.

In sickness or in health, let's remember that God is an all-knowing God that is all-loving. Therefore, he will never do anything that is not for our good. We do not have to question God. Instead, we should ask him to search our hearts. If we are being stretched too far, he knows our limits. God will never test us beyond what we are able to bear. The Christian life is not easy, but he is faithful. Nothing is too hard for him. Let's glorify him through his grace! "What is impossible with men is possible with God" (Luke 18:27). Learning to live every moment is God's presence is my goal.

Personal Response

1. Keep in mind God's character rather than his creation
2. God is Awesome.
3. Learn to live in the 'shadow' of God.
4. Be intimate in fellowship with Jesus Christ as Lord.
5. Chew on God's promises.
6. Grace is a part of glory.

Transformation

Learning to live every moment in God's presence requires transformation. Life becomes a celebration as I learn to follow Jesus. This is impossible without a relationship with him. Jesus had several conversations in the following verses. They were from different experiences, educations, interests, and cultures. His conversation had a special topic of interest. He always adapted his discussion to fit the person he was talking to. I am going to give our Savior's explanation for spiritual transformation. If I am going to characterize Jesus, I must have Jesus in my life (John 3).

Spiritual transformation involves, believing in not only the miracles or signs that Jesus performed to give authenticity to his person, but a full acceptance of his claim and commands. Jesus knows if we believe or not. He knows the heart of man and can evaluate our faith. What is spiritual transformation? It is the internal change (I Corinthians 5:17) of a person' nature through God's grace. Faith is the process for Jesus to enter and dwell in our hearts (Ephesians 3:17). There should be no confusion, camouflage, cover-up or stumbling.

In Jesus' own words, he declares what the gospel is all about and gives us as explanation. He says that we cannot enter the kingdom of God without becoming a new person. A complete change is compared to a rebirth. The natural man cannot enter into God's kingdom. The word is the text 'cannot' imply incapability rather than prohibition. Spiritual transformation has to take place. How can change take place? The pattern of life is set. Physical or psychological change is not the question. It has to do with the spiritual side of man. Jesus gives us these words, "except one be born of water and the Spirit, he cannot enter into the kingdom of God." In the word 'water' I discovered that acknowledgement of repentance and cleansing is necessary. A complete turn–around in body, soul, and spirit is necessary. To explain the word 'spirit', Jesus illustrates by using the word 'wind'. The wind's origin is undiscoverable, but his presence is manifested. Nobody can deny its existence. To be born by the Spirit means that the origin of life cannot be defined but it's actually can be seen by all.

How do I experience this new nature? Jesus continues by saying that new birth is a direct result of faith in his death and his resurrection power. Jesus of faith in his death and his resurrection power. Jesus gives God's attitude and purpose toward his world. He 'loved us' are words of the will rather than emotion. Belief is obedience to the voice of God; disobedience is unbelief. Belief is defined as commitment to authority rather than passive opinion.

We can come to Christ as a learned inquirer. We can come in and attitude of indifference. We can come as a result of desperation. The initial reason is insignificant. Accept God's love and place your trust in his Song and be spiritually transformed. God's presence involves transformation.

Personal Response

1. Rebirth starts transformation.

2. We must understand our nature.

3. Keep busy in glorifying God.

4. Hope is not built on emotional fantasy.

5. Accept God's commands and claims.

6. Informal change is necessary in faith.

Instruction

Learning to live every moment in God's presence requires applying his instruction. Out of all the promises I have learned, this one seems to cover all of them. As I draw near to him, he gives me the instruction I need to follow. He equips me to face whatever is before me. This provides the enablement and mindset needed to live a full and complete life (John 10:10). As he draws near to me, I am able to sense his presence. This provides confidence and joy in knowing that he has my best interest in mind even if I don't understand at the time.

I am going to share what I am practicing in order to overcome weakness, temptations, health issues, decision making and just plain troublesome issues. Someone said, "thinking right aways precedes acting right." I would add spiritual insight and application will cause us to think right and act right. I have discovered that the promises work. Put into action Jesus' words and you will find contentment and rest.

"Draw near to me and I will draw near to you" is found in James 4:8. James, the brother of Jesus, was used through the Holy Spirit to pen these words. James was ministering in Jerusalem. The church was persecuted and driven out of the city and scattered, He says do not be alarmed or sad. The child of God may rejoice victoriously even in the darkest hour. To rejoice I have to not only obtain knowledge (the facts) but it involves experiential knowledge (doing). Most of all, it involves an illumined heart (Holy Spirit counsel). I am excited to know what when I do not get it (the answer for difficult issues), I can always ask for wisdom (1:5). I can find purpose in the predicament. I am not going to doubt God. He has given me faith and I trust the faith giver. God is all he claims to be.

I have to learn to listen to his Word and then do it. I have to learn to be submissive and live life with spiritual discernment. I have to learn to practice self-control. God's grace is at work. Practicing submission to God and resisting the enemy will pave the way for me to draw near to God and assure me of him drawing near to me.

Drawing near to God involves as attitude of helplessness which will result in enablement. In Jesus' own words, he says "Blessed are the poor in spirit for theirs is the Kingdom of heaven." (Matthew 5:3). He gives the instruction on how to draw near and he gives the source of power behind it. I have to come to the realization that dependance upon God is necessary. I have to acknowledge sin in my life. I have to receive and believe in Jesus Christ (Acts 16:31; Romans 10:9-1-). His enablement takes place when a relationship develops with him, and I lean what 'thy will be done on earth as it is in heaven" means on a daily basis. I have a double citizenship on earth and heaven. My life is nothing less that "Christ in you, the hope of glory" (Colossians

1:27). Natural life has a beginning but no end. My eternal life will provide fellowship with God for all eternity. My life on earth is preparation for heaven and drawing closer to him.

Helplessness refers to not being able to help oneself. To be "poor in spirit" means that I have emptied myself of me—now there is room to be filled. The world promotes self-sufficiency or at the present time (2010) government sufficiency, yet God dwells with the man whose heart is broken (Isaiah 57:15). When this secession is made, the promise of inheriting the Kingdom will provide enablement. Power, energy, and strength are found in the centerpiece of God's attributes "Hallowed be thy name" (Matthew 6:9). This opens up a whole dimension of reverence, respect, awe, appreciation, honor, glory adoration, and worship. To hallow God's name means to hold his matchless being in reverence so that we will believe what he says and will obey him. When I live by faith and bear fruit in my character, I will exalt God's name. God has asked me to live in harmony with who he is and has stated this in his

Word. I must understand my helplessness and promised enablement. When I fear God, I will have the necessary ingredient of life which opens the door to everything good (Psalm 111:10; Proverbs 1:7,8,13).

I know through personal experience God's enablement through helplessness. I can talk about sickness (heart disease, cancer) and about several friends with a variety of physical or mental illnesses. I can share about financial stress and looking for a job without success. I can include inferiority complex and the lack of confidence—the list is long.

Enablement comes through understanding the Biblical phrase "It is he that hath made us and we are his" (Psalm 100:3). I have seen this positive phrase bring spiritual enablement for many besides myself. We can be assured in our total dependence upon him that it will provide authority because he is all powerful. I cannot Lord, but you can. Abiding in Jesus is the secret of enablement.

Drawing near to God involves an attitude of repentance which will result in comfort. In Jesus' own words he says, "Blessed are they that mourn for they shall be comforted" (Matthew 5:4). He also says in his model prayer "thy kingdom come," heavenly comfort will come to us (Matthew 6:10). He gives the source of power behind it.

I have come to the realization that repentance is necessary if I am going to draw near to hm. I have asked myself often, "do I ever mourn for sin that has been allowed in my life; do I experience anguish over lost souls, and the disobedience of followers of Jesus?" I know that I can experience God's compassion through my repentance and be renewed.

Mourning refers to a sincere sorrow for sin. God hats sin. I should also. It grieves him but I like to make excuses for it. Tolerance, deception, and like to make excuses for it. Tolerance, deception, and blindness—add your own favorite word to the list that creates a blockage to growth. Repentance means a change of mind. It is a gift of God (Acts 5:31; 11:18; Romans 2:4). I have to be mournful not only because of the consequences of sin and the baseness of sin but also the divine compassion provided in salvation.

Repentance will challenge me to put the Scripture into action. "Put to death—whatever belongs to your earthly nature" (Colossians 3:5). Sometimes I forget my responsibility. I have to make a personal decision to pursue holiness. I have to learn to put to death the misdeeds of my body. I have to destroy the strength and vitality of sin as it tries to reign in my body. Just think of it—my body is the temple of the Holy Spirit. He will do it. He is sufficient for this work. Conviction will start the path toward a holy life. Keep in mind "without holiness no one will see the Lord" (Hebrews 12:14) I want to be drawn near to God.

The world's values that are everywhere present must be replaced with God's. I have to let God remake me and not allow the world to squeeze me in (Romans 12:2). I have learned that only through God's Word can my mind be renewed. It takes conviction and obedience linked together with confession will bring comfort in my repentance. Confession is necessary every day.

God hates sin, and I must be sensitive to it. I must confess it and accept God's comfort in my repentance. I must let his Word work in my life. I must hide his Word in my heart. I have used the word "must" several times. It is important to do what I am trying to emphasize or I will fail. To understand what is right or wrong to do, I have to ask myself, "is helpful physically, spiritually and mentally? Does it glorify God?" (I Corinthians 6:12; 8:13; 10:31).

Drawing near to God involves an attitude of surrender which will result in a controlled life. In Jesus' own words he said, "Blessed are the meek for they shall inherit the earth" (Matthew5). He also said in his model prayer "thy will be done on earth as it is in heaven" this meekness is characterized in heaven (Matthew 6:10). He gives the instruction and how to draw near, and he gives the source of power behind it. I have come to the realization that meekness in my life will bring about a controlled life. Meekness refers to living for the glory of God. There is no room for self-will. It is not thinking of asserting my own rights. Meekness is brought into my life through God's grace. I have to learn to accept God's dealing with me without resistance or dispute. No more rebelling or fighting against God. It flows form the heart of humility and submission.

I believe that when I have the three 'Thys' in the right perspective in my life (found in Jesus' model prayer), I will experience the meekness characteristic I am glad that the Holy Spirit makes this possible (Romans 8:26,27). I have to practice faith and the certainty of the Holy Spirit's indwelling. I have to surrender my will to his will. I have to place Jesus' name on everything. The word 'thy' emphasizes God's rule. His sovereignty is in charge. He has absolute control over all of creation. I have to live life in relationship with his sovereignty. I don't have to figure out the plan.

The sovereign kingdom rule has to be followed. Meekness and control are the fruit of obedience. I have to learn to switch on the confidence button by turning to God and away from sin, switch on the confidence button by allowing my inner judge of moral issues to be in tune with Jesus Christ, switch on the confidence button by making decisions through a righteous common sense, and switch on the confidence button by obeying the special assignment given to me. "The Kingdom of God is not meat and drink but righteousness, peace, and joy in the Holy Ghost" (Romans 14:17).

Drawing near to God involves an attitude of craving which will result in satisfaction. In Jesus's own words he says, "Blessed are they that hunger and thirst after righteousness for they shall be filled" (5:4). He also says in his model prayer "Give us this day our daily bread" (Matthew 6:10). He gives the instruction on how to draw near and he gives the source of power behind it. I have to come to the realization that craving after righteousness is absolutely necessary. Only when this takes place will I find contentment.

When I have a craving for something, I cannot leave it alone. It has a driving force behind it. It pushes me forward. This can be a good thing that takes place yet also bad. I am looking at the positive side and not the negative. Proof of my spiritual rebirth is found in my desire to pursue after righteousness with hunger and thirst. The inner passion is a blessing. Being poor/helpless/ being mournful/repentant, and being meek/ surrendered will cause a deep earnest desire to search the Scripture. This will bring satisfaction, appetite for good food is a good thing. What I eat will reveal the man I really am.

Craving after righteousness will take place as I study his Word. A few week ago, I was looking at some of my previous sermons. They are bound into a dozen or so books. I found one based upon Psalm 119:33-40—"quicken me in thy righteousness." The word 'quicken' means in

Hebrew to make alive, to refresh and in English it refers to a thought activating the thoughts in verses 33-40 that they will produce a craving heart for righteousness. "Teach me" (v.33) indicates that a foundation has been laid. The master teacher has brought the lesson to my ears and has establishes my way. The teaching has made me alive. "Give me understanding' (v.34) has brought discernment and correct insight. It is not only information and knowledge but a diligence to pursue it. Understanding has made me alive. "I delight in the path" (v.35), receiving the instruction, understanding the Word and careful observation has brought pleasure. A deep affection has been cultivated and has made me alive. "Incline my heart" (v.36); though God's testimonies, my being has been made alive. With the right purpose in mind, the attitude is covet Jesus Christ. "Turn away" (v.37) allows my eyes to feast upon Jesus and not my own vanity. Help me to move in the right direction and be made alive. "Establish thy Word" (v.38): my heart has been made alive through the respect and reverence that has integrated into my soul for Jesus.

"Turn away my reproach" (v.39); I have learned that your Word is sound, beneficial, righteous, fruitful, and pleasant. I have been made alive because your judgements are good. "Behold, I have longed after thy precepts" (v.40); craving for righteousness will be produced through an intense, sensitive, and energetic response to God's Word. I have to realize the source of quickening is through the infusion of the Holy Spirit. I have to realize that I have to respond to his quickening. I have to make a decision to feed upon the scripture. I am not a victim of worldliness or my own weaknesses. "Quicken thou me in thy way." This is possible because of Jesus' model prayer. He said, "give us this day our daily bread" (Matthew 6:11). This refers to all of my physical needs. When I am dependent upon him, he provides all my needs. Boldness is the Holy Spirit and confidence will empower me. I am thankful for the fact that he provides food, clothes, shelter, and especially his presence in health or sickness. I have discovered this in his Word that has power to quicken me.

Drawing near to God involves an attitude of empathy which will result in mercy. In Jesus' own words he says, "Blessed are the merciful for they shall obtain mercy" (Matthew 5:7). He also says in his model prayer "Forgive us our debts as we forgive our debtors" (Matthew 6:12). He gives the instruction on how to draw near and he gives the source of power behind it. I have come to the realization that experiencing empathy will bring mercy.

Mercy is defined as being compassionate. Compassion is having a feeling of deep sympathy. Sympathy is ability to share the feelings of another. This leads to empathy. Empathy is identifying with an experience of the feeling and thoughts of another. Someone told me that it is like getting in the skin of another. Mercy becomes a part of my life because I have obtained mercy. Jesus himself became a part of my life because I have obtained mercy. The Holy Spirit produces mercy. Jesus himself became the ultimate example of this when he cried from the cross, "Father, forgive them for they know not what they do" (Luke 23:34).

When I get in touch with God, I can feel his mercy at work on my behalf. It started when I trusted in him (Ephesians 2:4-7) and he gave me a clean heart (Acts 15:9) and peace within (Romans 5:1). When I receive mercy, I then can share his mercy with others. I pray that I can be sensitive to others that cross my path. I hope I can sense their hopelessness and need. I desire to come alongside of them.

Drawing near to God involves an attitude of authenticity which will result in seeing God. In Jesus' own words he says "Blessed are the pure in heart for they shall see God" (Matthew 5:8). He also says in his model prayer "and lead us not into temptation but deliver us" (Matthew 6:13). He gives the instruction, and he gives to the realization that purity will cause my heart to see God.

God is doing a work in me. He is conforming me into the image of Christ (Romans 8:29) whose image consists in "righteousness and true holiness" (Ephesians 4:24). Purity of heart is a part of my election and redemption (Ephesians 1:4; Titus 2:14). This is not sinlessness (I John 1:8) but the truth within (Psalm 51:6). It means a single heart. I am not divided between God and the world. I realize that this calls for radical living. The world praises pride not humility. The world endorses sin. The world is at war with God. Righteousness will cause persecution. Conflict will take place. Since my life has been transformed by the grace of God, I will see him. Daily faith will bring me into his presence. I might be called peculiar (Titus 2:14) but I have been chosen by the Father, purchased by the Son and sealed by the Spirit. I will see God.

Drawing near to God involves an attitude of harmony which will result in being called children of God. In Jesus' own words he said "blessed are the peacemakers for they will be called children of God" (Matthew 5:9). He gives the instruction and how to draw near and he gives the source of power behind it. I have come to the realization that harmony with God will bring peace. With the regeneration power of the gospel in my life, I have experienced peace with God's message of peace to a troubled world because I daily experience the peace of God in my life. My ministry is to be a channel of God's mercy, purity, and peace.

There have been many times that I have stood between enemies. The Holy Spirit apparently was present to protect me. My attitude of peace caused such a stir and confusion that those enemies didn't know what to do. They would lay down their fists and with humility say, "what should we do?" That gave me opportunity to share the true peacemaker.

Drawing near to God involves an attitude of the Kingdom of heaven. "Blessed are they which are persecuted for righteousness sake" (Matthew 5:10). He also said in his model prayer "for thine is the power and the glory forever" (Matthew 6:13). He gives the instruction and how to draw near and he gives the source of power behind it. I have come to the realization that if persecuted, I am assured of the Kingdom of heaven. The Bible says, "yea and all that will live godly in Christ Jesus shall suffer persecution" (2 Timothy 3:12). I know that suffering can be experienced through being kept from ones through being tempted through social enterprise. I know suffering can be produced by fellow Christians. Someday I may experience suffering through physical abuse.

I can experience his power, presence, and peace (Psalm 16:8). The key to spiritual victory is to stay close to God. I have to learn to practice God's presence all day long. "The Lord is near to all who call on him" (Psalm 145:18). The songwriter has written "have thine own way Lord." During persecution and peace, I am going to celebrate life in magnifying Jesus' name.

Jesus never promised ease to those of us he called to follow him. Reliance upon Jesus will cause radical living. Ridicule will most likely pursue us but keep in mind a reward will follow. Jesus lived through persecution, he died through persecution, and he rose again after the persecution.

Drawing near to God will fulfill God's promise that he will draw near to me. When I apply Jesus' instruction and experience his power through his model prayer, the Holy Spirt will produce his fruit in my life. The word "blessed" (Matthew 5:1-12) truthfully becomes a description of my life.

I have come to the end of this study and yet I have to return to the beginning with the word "blessed". Blessed means happy. My inner being is happy because of the work of God in my life. The characteristics I have been sharing have been a result of believing.

- I am learning to be helpless (poor in spirit).
- I am learning to be repentive (mournful).
- I am leaning to be surrendered (meek).
- I am learning to crave (hunger).
- I am learning to practice empathy (mercy).
- I am learning to be authentic (pure).

- I am learning to be in harmony (peacemaker).
- I am learning to be victorious in suffering (Persecution).

I am blessed with the Holy Spirit's enablement to experience a "touch of heaven" here on earth through practicing these attributes. I am realizing God's rule and providence in my life on earth. I am looking forward to when the last enemy (sin and death) (I Corinthians 15:24-28) will be destroyed at the Lord's return.

I am drawing near to him every day as I practice the Lord's instructions. The day will come when he will draw near to me even with greater intensity. "Face to face, I will behold him, far beyond the starry sky, Face to face, in all his glory, I shall see him by and by!? The only condition is faith in God's Son, the Lord Jesus Christ. He said. "For God so loved the world that he gave his only begotten son, that whoever believes on him should not perish but have everlasting life" (John 3:16).

I love my home here on earth. A day does not go by that as I walk in the yard with my dogs that I don't forget to thank God for the beauty and pleasantness of the place he has given me to live. I realize that my happiness is wherever my family is, that's home. As I draw near to God and he draw near to me, I can call heaven my eternal home. Death does not end all. My Spirit lives on and enters immediately into the very presence of God.

Death involves physical and spiritual separation. Physical death occurs when my spirit is separated from the body. Spiritual death is the eternal separation of the spirit from God. This means that as a believer, I will never be separated from God. Jesus said "He who hears my word and believes in him who sent me has everlasting life" (John 5:24). In the deepest sense of the word, I will never die. Jesus gave the promise, "whoever lives and believes in me shall never die" (John 11:25,26). Jesus is my source of life. He is the resurrection and the life. My life between death and resurrection will be a time of joy, blessing, and fellowship with Jesus. Drawing near to him starts a deep and sweet relationship that will continue into a greater depth in heaven.

I am learning to live my life with a double citizenship. I am glad that I am a citizen of the United States of America and also of the heavenly city. A day is coming when our present solar system will be burned with fire and will be replaced by a new heaven and a new earth (2 Peter 3:10). It will burst into flames with such intense heat that even that elements that make up matter will be dissolved. The sun, the moon, the planets, and the distant stars will all be engulfed in flames, but this will not be a tragedy. The Bible says that out of the ruins will emerge a glorious new world—my eternal home (Revelation 21:1,2).

As I draw near to God and he draws near to me, he will bring me into a wonderful life. In my eternal home, which is a perfect society, I will realize my full spiritual potential as an induvial. I will enter in an eternal fellowship with God. An endless variety of meaningful activities will take place. All imperfections of this life will be gone, and positive blessings will be in abundance. My present knowledge of God, while real and precious, is incomplete. In heaven I will know him perfectly. I will behold the glory of his presence and faith will turn to sight (Revelation 21:3).

If my attitude is based upon a submission and obedience, God will draw near to me. He says, "I will draw near to you." This gives me a sense of his presence and love. To understand God's love, I have to know God's eternal passion to accomplish his will in such a way that he is glorified. God's love is eternal. God was love before he created man or anything else. I have to learn to let God be God. His will and glory go hand in hand to produce his move. I am under his umbrella of love. He unfolds his will to achieve his glory in my life through love.

The ultimate definition of God's love is expressed in these words: action, sacrifice, beneficial, unconditional. and emotional. I must keep his purpose in mind and then inner strength will flow.

He says, "I will draw near to you." This gives me a sense of his presence and grace. I do not deserve grave, but God has given it to me. It is his unmerited favor. Grace is designed to save me and keep me. The Scripture says, "Grow in the grace and knowledge of our Lord and Savior Jesus Christ." (2 Peter 3:18). God is sufficient. God's grace is his empowerment to overcome. It raises me above the problem and gives me power at the exact point when I want to quit. Grace instructs me in how to live. Grace gives victory where I didn't' have it. Grace will give the ability to keep going. Grace is the exchanging of my life in me (Galatians 5:1). I am challenged to measure my growth in grace; if I am lacking, I ask for his grace (Galatians 5:22,23).

He says, "I will draw near to you." This gives me a sense of his presence and glory. God's inner core is a radiating light (I Timothy 6: 15, 16). God's visible glory was most fully seen in the person of Jesus Christ (John 1:1, 14, 18). Jesus

Christ is God in the flesh (Matthew 17:1-8). I am to tell of his glory (Psalm 96:1-3). His glory will put a glow in my life. Transformation is a growing adventure. I have to learn to submit to God's glory (I Corinthians 10:31). I glorify him when I . . .

- Show Christ like character (John 15:8)
- Apply Biblical truths (Matthew 5:16)
- Practice sexual purity (I Corinthians 6:18-20)
- Daily confession of sins (Joshua 7:19)
- Live by faith (Romans 4:19-21)
- Proclaim his Word (2 Thessalonians 3:1)
- Do his will (John 17:41)
- Confess his Son (Philippians 2:10)

He says, "I will draw near to you." This gives, me a sense of his presence and justice. God is good, kind, loving, and forgiving. He is also just, and I must take his wrath seriously. God must judge sin because of the justice of his law and the righteousness of his character. He takes no pleasure in punishing the unrighteous (Ezekiel 33:11). He will judge all men according to their deeds (I Peter 1:17). The word "wrath" indicates God's intense displeasure of sin. God's wrath is not cruel but just. There are two sides to God's response to sin. "Thou hast loved righteousness and hated wickedness" (Psalm 45:7). I am glad that God is patient (2 Peter 3:9). My only way of escape is through God's substitute, Jesus who "delivers me from the wrath to come" (I Thessalonians 1:10).

Christ died for me (Romans 5:8,9).

He says, "I will draw near to you." This gives me a sense of his presence and wisdom. Wisdom is knowing that God's purpose is to glorify himself. Wisdom moves all events, all people, and all circumstances towards his purpose. Whether I resist or cooperate, he is still going to achieve his purpose. Wisdom is the ability to use my spiritual character, Biblical knowledge, common sense, and circumstances and blending them together. I have an infinitely wise God that tells me to ask him for wisdom. I am not where I am by luck or chance. The infinitely wise God has been ordering my life.

I was in his mind before the creation of earth. He will give wisdom to make the response that will bring him glory. A determined will to agree with "thy will be done" is the answer. Ask in faith and anticipate the answer. Mixing human wisdom and divine wisdom doesn't work (James 3:16-18). To obtain wisdom, I have to admit that I need it. I have to stand in awe of God (Psalm 111:10). I have to study the Word. I need to pray for wisdom (James 1:5).

I will draw need to God. I have accepted the challenge and have followed his instruction through his "blessed sayings" and his model prayer with intensity.

Personal Response

1. Practice faith in daily life
2. Obtain knowledge—facts
3. Experience knowledge–doing
4. Understand illumination—Holy Spirit
5. Jesus never promised ease
6. Practice God's prayer model

Solution

I am in the process of learning that "Discovering God's Presence" in every moment is necessary if I am going to live with vitality and vibrancy. This is not a backward or illogical approach in finding God. It provides an absolute encounter with God through Jesus Christ (Biblical Christianity).

Have you discovered yourself described with these faithless words? Discouragement—dismay—disconnectedness—distress—dejection—depression

They are chasing me with cancer, heart disease, and internal issues, but guess what? I have found a solution. It has started with a little sacred phrase that will produce an abundant life- "He made me, and I am His" (Psalm

100:3). This phrase is found in the middle of a doxology found in Psalm 100. It is a beautiful poetic Psalm of praise. As a musician/educator, I love the Psalm because it begins with "make a joyful noise." In my, music conducting and teaching. I spend a lot of time trying to move that 'noise' into a joyful musical rendition. I know the scriptural text emphasizes a 'shout of worship.' It is like a crescendo in music, flowing free with joy and thanksgiving as we worship him.

The Psalmist's invitation to enter joyfully into God's presence has provided the phrase "He made me, and I am His." I have learned to translate that phrase into God's power, presence, and peace. In today's language of reinforcement, I have applied it to my life with strength, support, and steadfastness. "My hope is in Jesus . . . hear my prayer O, Lord, listen to my cry for help" (Psalm 39:7,12). I know victory will come because God keeps to his word. The process begins with decisions and making some adjustments. I have to find the right resource.

I have discovered my best and most qualified resource is found in Jesus Christ (Isaiah 9:6).

The "he is Psalm 100:3 refers to Jesus. He is God and man. He is divine and human. He is infinite and finite. "A son is given" emphasizes his humanity. I am learning to trade my self-centeredness for God-centered faith. It is a realization of less of me and more of him. I find comfort, confidence, and courage in this absolute truth. I am reminded that my resource is God himself.

His name is wonderful. Can I say that Christ lives in me? (Galatians 2:20). Intimate fellowship is necessary, and this requires belief in God (Acts 16:31) and continues with knowing him (Philippians 3:7,8). My companion is Jesus Christ. Transformation has taken place. The miracle of the new birth has been made possible through his name.

His name is counselor. Can I respond to his advice? He is qualified to counsel. He is eternal God "whom dwelleth with the fullness of the

Godhead bodily" (Colossians 2:9). He knows my thought process (Ezekiel 11:5). God is concerned about details. He knows everything that is going on behind the scenes (Job 23:10).

His name is mighty God. Can I trust him? Jesus is God himself. There is nothing God cannot do. He says be strong in the Lord and in the strength of his might (Ephesians 6:10). He takes care of the demands of life. No matter what the problem he has power to meet it, handle it, solve it, and use it for my good and his glory.

His name is everlasting. Can I accept his sovereignty? He is eternal. With him I live in a dimension of life. God has absolute rule and control over all things (Psalm 24:1). There is more to life than what my senses reveal. I am safe in Jesus because of who he is. I can trust his big picture for me.

His name is Prince of Peace. Can I make the adjustments? An alignment with God is necessary. The process is through his grace. Do not try to change the circumstances but change in character. Peace comes from inside out. His love brings a win-win situation.

His name is Lord. Can I obey his rule? All future government shall be upon his shoulder. Authentic transformation takes place when I seek him first in obedience and surrender. He is in charge and in control. I am surrounded with his infinite person, power, and glory (John 14:20). I have a union with him.

He made me and I am his. My resource is found in Jesus Christ. My remedy is in identifying the 'me' (Psalm 100:3). I have to discover who I am, and then I have to act upon it. I am, and then I have to act upon it. I am a new creation in Jesus Christ (2 Corinthians 5:17). The 'therefore' refers to the flesh. I do not have to think in the flesh any longer. I have a sacred union with Jesus. A spiritual birth has taken place. I have been born form above. I am in the kingdom of God. This life comes through belief in Jesus. When the favorite text of many people goes into action (John 3:16), the witness of the Holy Spirit is available (I John 5:10).

I am Jesus Christ's workmanship. The word workmanship means that which is made. God is making me like Jesus (Romans 8:29). Christianity is progressive. It is a developmental process. He is equipping me through:

1. The Word of God (I Thessalonians 2:13; I Corinthians 2:9-13). The word will cleanse me, nourish me and lead me.

2. Prayer (Ephesians 3:20-21)—the power of God is released through my intimate fellowship and communion with God.

3. Suffering (I Peter 4:11-14) the Holy Spirit will come alongside of me to provide strength, security, and steadfast.

I am dependent on Jesus Christ (John 15:5). A continuous relationship is necessary. If I follow the daily routine of recitation, reflection, reliance, restoring, remembrance, and rejoicing, I will abide in Jesus and prevail. Th process does work.

He made me and I am his. I have thought about my resource, my remedy, and now my response. The word 'his' makes this phrase from God very personal. I have been chosen by the Father, purchased by the Son, and sealed by the Spirit. The 'he' has taught me through "his" model prayer to communicate to him. Prayer is the divine arrangement that God has made for me to communicate with him. The prayer brings it all together. "Thy name, thy will, thy kingdom come" is my response.

I have had to practice the presence of God. I have had to learn that my daily activities are directed by God's sovereignty and majesty. To be in attitude of prayer should be my continuous thought pattern. The model prayer is divided into a relationship, reverence, request, response, and rule.

"Thy name" gives me the rule I should follow in prayer. I have to ask in his name. To pray in his name means that I place Jesus' name in each request. Through the process, I will begin to understand what he desires for me. The reception of Christ is necessary. Confidence of the indwelling Spirit is necessary. Following Christ's example is necessary.

"Thy kingdom" gives me the rule I should follow in prayer. God sits on the throne of the universe as Lord. Living in his sovereign kingdom rule will give me strength. I can do anything when I am totally dependent upon his supply. The negatives and positives are both a part of his plan. The circumstances are under his direct control. There are no chance happenings, no mistakes and no accidents. God is arranging circumstances in my life to accomplish his purpose. I do not have to figure out the plan. I need to obey God with deep reverence for he is working within me working within me (Philippians 2:12,13). The kingdom refers to Christ reigning in my heart and living in a conscious awareness of his presence.

"Thy will" gives me the rule I should follow in prayer. His will is for me to yield my will to him. My responsibility is to submit to his authority and trust him. The Bible is the absolute standard of faith and practice. God gives me both intellect and emotion to cooperate with my will in doing his will (Psalm 119:66).

I have to make this personal. His scripture and prayer will make it possible for me to dare to begin to trust my thoughts and feelings. His hallowed name and his kingdom rule gives him right to predetermine the plan of the universe. God knows the end from the beginning. God will do what God will do. My responsibility is to submit to his authority, obey his commands, and trust him. This is how faith becomes real. I will "Discover God's Presence" as I commit to a deeper life in Christ.

Personal Response

1. Learn to translate power, presence, and peace into reality
2. Believe Biblical Christianity
3. Be filled by the Holy Spirit.
4. Define the difference between old and new nature
5. Learn to search Biblical solutions
6. Discover hope in faith

Responsibility

I know humanity can be messed up. I know some people are full of deception. They find themselves in the company with Adam and Eve. They have lost their freedom because of disobedience and the fall. They choose to follow their own will rather than God's will (Genesis 1-3). I know some people have in foolishness decided to concentrate their efforts on having earthly treasures rather than heavenly (Matthew 6:33). I know some people have been just simply full of confusion. A constant warfare in the battle (Romans 7:14-24). My meditation method will achieve its purpose with the correct conditions. These requirements have to be accomplished.

Four decisions need to be made. Conversion is a decision to receive. God is the initiator of salvation. I am called (I Peter 2:9), chosen (Ephesians 1:4), saved (I Timothy 1:9), and justified (Romans 8:30) through him. I receive him through believing (John 1:12, 3:16). May I be very clear? I have to make a confession of faith (Romans 10:9-10). This means I agree that belief in the saving power of the risen Christ must come from the innermost part of my being. Cleansing is the next decision. It is to separate oneself form sin (I John 1:9). Sin is when I miss God's standard. I have to acknowledge the wrong pattern of living that I practice. Genuine salvation is demonstrated through being sensitive to sin. Consecration is a decision to surrender (Romans 12:1-2). I have to dedicate my life to Jesus Christ. He is '**ABOVE ALL**'. My top priority is to model my life after him. It has to be a define act. It is a response to faith. Yielding my body totally to God is necessary. I am in the process of being transformed. My helper has changed my inner nature and has become my sovereign controller.

Claiming is a decision to accept (John 12:48). I have to put into action all the decisions. Then I must claim the promise, or I will miss the abundant life (John 10:10). The four decisions will meet the condition to have the correct desire to allow the meditation model to work. In summary, the conditions are a fulfillment of Ephesians 5:18, "be filled with the Holy Spirit".

Personal Response

1. We are in Christ Jesus through faith
2. Choose to follow Biblical truth.
3. Don't allow humanity to be messed up.
4. Don't follow confusion.
5. Understand conversion, cleansing
6. Communication and Comfort

Strategy

Here is a sample of the routine to follow:

1. I have to accept the proper **RESOURCE**.
2. I have to absorb the text into my mind through **RECITATION**.
3. I have to analyze the promise with clarity and **REFLECTION**.
4. I have to allow it to make the decisions in my life which will bring **RELIANCE**.
5. I have to accept the truth to renew my spirit through **RESTORATION**.
6. I have to affirm the positive and negative thoughts to **REMEMBER**.
7. I have to abide in Christ as I **REJOICE** in victory.

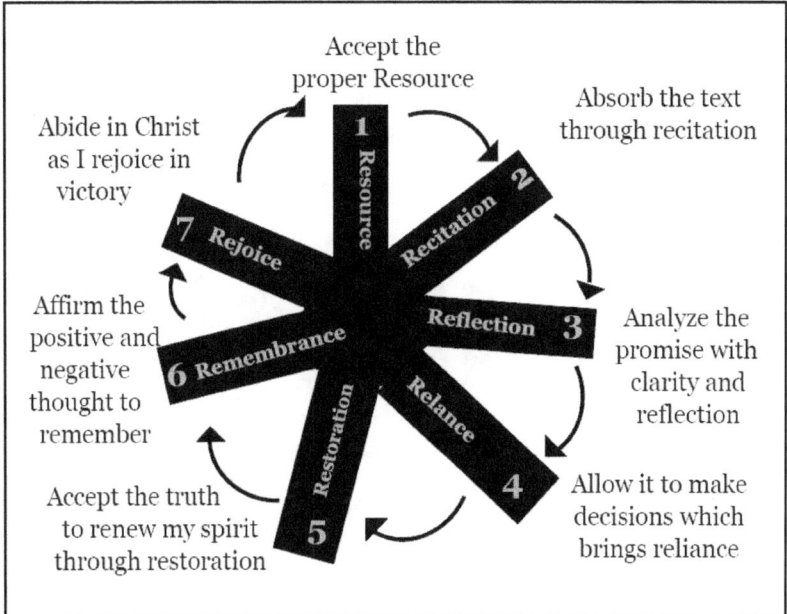

- God has used John greatly in ministry and will continue to use him through this life giving series.

- As John sees God working in his life and in the lives of those to whom he ministers his is refreshed.

- His books give us hope and light. It gives encouragement. It provides a growth process.

- His book gives supported truths that have been practiced in a deep relationship with Jesus Christ.

- We need the Pastoral Health Care Series. Dr. John Gillette's ministries come from a life walked with God.

www.ingramcontent.com/pod-product-compliance
Lightning Source LLC
Chambersburg PA
CBHW061706120626
46550CB00003B/1113